Maths
made easy

Key Stage 2
ages 9-10
Beginner

Author John Kennedy
Consultant Sean McArdle

Certificate

Congratulations to ....
(write your name here)
for successfully finishing this book.

 You're a star!

DK

LONDON • NEW YORK • MUNICH • MELBOURNE • DELHI

Partition numbers to 10 000 000

How many hundreds are the same as 7 000?   *70*   hundreds
(70 x 100 = 7 000)

What is the nine worth in 694?   *90*   (because the nine digit
is in the 10s column)

How many tens are the same as:

400	tens	600	tens	900	tens
200	tens	1 300	tens	4 700	tens
4 800	tens	1 240	tens	1 320	tens
2 630	tens	5 920	tens	4 350	tens

What is the 7 worth in these numbers?

| 76 | 720 | 137 |
| 7 122 | 74 301 | 724 |

What is the 3 worth in these numbers?

| 324 126 | 3 927 141 | 214 623 |
| 8 254 320 | 3 711 999 | 124 372 |

How many hundreds are the same as:

6 400	hundreds	8 500	hundreds
19 900	hundreds	36 200	hundreds
524 600	hundreds	712 400	hundreds

What is the 8 worth in these numbers?

| 8 214 631 | 2 398 147 | 463 846 |
| 287 034 | 8 110 927 | 105 428 |

Multiplying and dividing by 10

Write the answer in the box.

37 x 10 =   *370*   58 ÷ 10 =   *5.8*

Write the answer in the box.

94 x 10 =   13 x 10 =   37 x 10 =

36 x 10 =   47 x 10 =   54 x 10 =

236 x 10 =   419 x 10 =   262 x 10 =

531 x 10 =   674 x 10 =   801 x 10 =

Write the answer in the box.

92 ÷ 10 =   48 ÷ 10 =   37 ÷ 10 =

18 ÷ 10 =   29 ÷ 10 =   54 ÷ 10 =

345 ÷ 10 =   354 ÷ 10 =   723 ÷ 10 =

531 ÷ 10 =   262 ÷ 10 =   419 ÷ 10 =

Find the number that has been multiplied by 10.

____ x 10 = 230   ____ x 10 = 750   ____ x 10 = 990

____ x 10 = 480   ____ x 10 = 130   ____ x 10 = 250

____ x 10 = 520   ____ x 10 = 390   ____ x 10 = 270

____ x 10 = 620   ____ x 10 = 860   ____ x 10 = 170

Find the number that has been divided by 10.

____ ÷ 10 = 4.7   ____ ÷ 10 = 6.8   ____ ÷ 10 = 12.4

____ ÷ 10 = 25.7   ____ ÷ 10 = 36.2   ____ ÷ 10 = 31.4

____ ÷ 10 = 40.8   ____ ÷ 10 = 67.2   ____ ÷ 10 = 80.9

____ ÷ 10 = 92.4   ____ ÷ 10 = 32.7   ____ ÷ 10 = 56.3

Ordering sets of amounts

Write these amounts in order, starting with the smallest.

3 100 km	24 km	1 821 km	247 km	4 km	960 km

4 km   24 km   247 km   960 km   1 821 km   3 100 km

Write these amounts in order, starting with the smallest.

£526	£15 940	£1 504	£826	£37 532

720 m	7 200 m	27 410 m	15 m	247 m

70 000 l	650 l	26 000 l	6 500 l	7 000 l

656 kg	9 565 kg	22 942 kg	752 247 kg	1 327 kg

9 520 yrs	320 yrs	4 681 yrs	8 940 yrs	20 316 yrs

217 846 kg	75 126 kg	8 940 kg	14 632 kg	175 kg

9 420 km	764 km	25 811 km	114 243 km	7 240 km

£37 227	£1 365 240	£143 820	£950	£4 212

24 091 m	59 473 m	1 237 m	426 m	837 201 m

47 632 kg	847 kg	9 625 kg	103 427 kg	2 330 kg

7 340 m	249 m	12 746 m	32 m	17 407 321 m

Ordering sets with negative numbers

Write these numbers in order, starting with the smallest.

6	9	−3	5	−2	0

−3   −2   0   5   6   9

Put these numbers on the number line.

1	2	−1	−3	3	−4
		−2	0		4 5

```
├───┼───┼───┼───┼───┼───┼───┼───┼───┼───┤
```

Write these numbers in order, starting with the smallest.

7   3   −4   −1   6   4   −2   0   9   −5

10   3   −8   −7   9   −12   8   4   −2   −1

11   −7   3   −2   0   12   8   −2   −8   6

Do the same with these groups of numbers.

4   7   −3   −1   9   −4   1   −8   0   2

2   −8   0   5   −14   20   −18   7   −5   10

5   −3   0   −7   −1   11   −15   2   9   −4

−12   3   −7   8   25   −2   14   −9   12   −20

Counting in constant steps

Continue each row.

Steps of 6	−5	1	7	13	19	25	31
Steps of 3	7	4	1	−2	−5	−8	−11

Continue each row.

−20	−10	0			
−15	−10	−5			
−9	−7	−5			
−2	5	12			
−11	−8	−5		4	
−2	6	14	30		

Continue each row.

24	18	12		
13	9	5		
7	3	−1		
32	24	16		−8
35	28	21		
8	5	2		−10

Continue each row.

22	16	10	−2	
−4	5	14		
3	−2	−7		
17	10	3		−18
−1	2	5		

Recognising multiples

Circle the multiples of 10.

14   (20)   25   (30)   47   (60)

Circle the multiples of 6.

20	48	56	72	25	35
1	3	6	16	26	36

Circle the multiples of 7.

14	24	35	27	47	49
63	42	52	37	64	71

Circle the multiples of 8.

25	31	48	84	32	8
18	54	64	35	72	28

Circle the multiples of 9.

17	81	27	35	92	106
45	53	108	90	33	95
64	9	28	18	36	98

Circle the multiples of 10.

15	35	20	46	90	100
44	37	30	29	50	45

Circle the multiples of 11.

24	110	123	54	66	90
45	33	87	98	99	121
43	44	65	55	21	22

Circle the multiples of 12.

136	134	144	109	108	132
24	34	58	68	48	60
35	29	72	74	84	94

Factors of numbers from 31 to 65

The factors of 40 are   1   2   4   5   8   10   20   40

Circle the factors of 56.

(1)   (2)   3   (4)   5   6   (7)   (8)   (14)   (28)   32   (56)

Find all the factors of these numbers.

The factors of 31 are

The factors of 47 are

The factors of 60 are

The factors of 50 are

The factors of 42 are

The factors of 32 are

The factors of 48 are

The factors of 35 are

The factors of 52 are

Circle the factors of these numbers.

Which numbers are factors of 39?
1   2   3   4   5   8   9   10   13   14   15   20   25   39

Which numbers are factors of 45?
1   3   4   5   8   9   12   15   16   21   24   36   40   44   45

Which numbers are factors of 61?
1   3   4   5   6   10   15   16   18   20   26   31   40   61

Which numbers are factors of 65?
1   2   4   5   6   8   9   10   12   13   14   15   30   60   65

Some numbers only have factors of 1 and themselves. They are called prime numbers.
Write all the prime numbers between 31 and 65 in the box.

Square numbers

The square has two rows and two columns. It is 2^2.

How many dots are there?   4

2^2 is the same as
$2 \times 2 = 4$

Draw a picture like the one above to show each of these numbers.

3^2

How many
dots are there?

4^2

How many
dots are there?

5^2

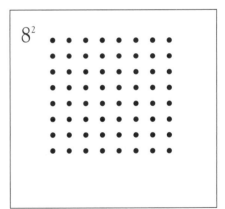

How many
dots are there?

6^2

How many
dots are there?

7^2

How many
dots are there?

8^2

How many
dots are there?

9^2

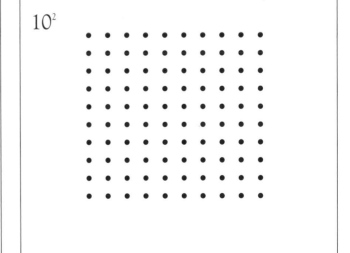

How many dots are there?

10^2

How many dots are there?

Finding fractions of amounts

Find $\frac{1}{2}$ of £25.00.

£25.00   ÷   2   =   £12.50   Remember that £12.5 is not correct.

Find $\frac{1}{10}$ of 3 cm.

3 cm   ÷   10   =   0.3 cm   or   30 mm ÷ 10 = 3 mm

0.3 cm is the same as 3 mm.

Find $\frac{1}{2}$ of these amounts.

24 cm	30p
£1.50	16 cm
14 hours	60 kg

Find $\frac{1}{4}$ of these amounts.

20 min	16 l
8 km	36 hours
48 g	24 cm

Find $\frac{1}{10}$ of these amounts.

5 cm	12 cm
£4.00	5 l
30p	9 kg
5 hours	6 km

Find $\frac{1}{100}$ of these amounts.

£40.00	50 cm
20 km	90 g
50 m	36 l
15 hours	£75.00

Changing simple fractions and decimals

Write these fractions as decimals.

$\frac{7}{10}$ = 0.7

$\frac{3}{100}$ = 0.03

Write these decimals as fractions.

0.2 = $\frac{2}{10}$ or $\frac{1}{5}$

0.47 = $\frac{47}{100}$

Write these fractions as decimals.

$\frac{3}{10}$

$\frac{2}{5}$

$\frac{1}{2}$

$\frac{7}{10}$

$\frac{1}{5}$

$\frac{1}{4}$

$\frac{9}{10}$

$\frac{3}{5}$

$\frac{3}{4}$

Write these decimals as fractions.

0.1 = $\frac{1}{}$

0.4 = $\frac{2}{}$

0.7 = $\frac{7}{}$

0.2 = $\frac{1}{}$

0.5 = $\frac{1}{}$

0.8 = $\frac{4}{}$

0.3 = $\frac{3}{}$

0.6 = $\frac{3}{}$

0.9 = $\frac{9}{}$

Change these fractions to decimals.

$\frac{1}{100}$

$\frac{15}{100}$

$\frac{24}{100}$

$\frac{3}{100}$

$\frac{25}{100}$

$\frac{56}{100}$

$\frac{7}{100}$

$\frac{49}{100}$

$\frac{72}{100}$

Change these decimals to fractions.

0.39 =

0.83 =

0.51 =

0.47 =

0.91 =

0.43 =

0.21 =

0.73 =

0.17 =

Adding two or three numbers

Work out the answer to each sum.

$$\begin{array}{r} 5\,241 \text{ km} \\ +\ 3\,527 \text{ km} \\ \hline 8768 \text{ km} \\ \hline \end{array}$$

$$\begin{array}{r} 2\,682 \text{ m} \\ 3\,220 \text{ m} \\ +\ 2\,314 \text{ m} \\ \hline 8216 \text{ m} \\ \hline 1\,1 \end{array}$$

Remember to carry if you need to.

Work out the answer to each sum.

$$\begin{array}{r} 1\,985 \text{ km} \\ +\ 2\,841 \text{ km} \\ \hline \\ \hline \end{array} \qquad \begin{array}{r} 5\,763 \text{ km} \\ +\ 3\,528 \text{ km} \\ \hline \\ \hline \end{array} \qquad \begin{array}{r} 6\,247 \text{ km} \\ +\ 1\,519 \text{ km} \\ \hline \\ \hline \end{array}$$

$$\begin{array}{r} 2\,640 \text{ km} \\ 1\,739 \text{ km} \\ +\ 2\,101 \text{ km} \\ \hline \\ \hline \end{array} \qquad \begin{array}{r} 3\,521 \text{ km} \\ 2\,195 \text{ km} \\ +\ 2\,325 \text{ km} \\ \hline \\ \hline \end{array} \qquad \begin{array}{r} 4\,813 \text{ km} \\ 2\,000 \text{ km} \\ +\ 3\,458 \text{ km} \\ \hline \\ \hline \end{array}$$

Write the answer in the box.

$2\,753 \text{ m} + 1\,375 \text{ m} =$ \qquad $4\,813 \text{ m} + 2\,427 \text{ m} + 1\,023 \text{ m} =$

$3\,714 \text{ m} + 5\,918 \text{ m} =$ \qquad $2\,349 \text{ m} + 1\,773 \text{ m} + 3\,859 \text{ m} =$

Put the missing numbers in these sums.

$$\begin{array}{r} 6\,4\,2 \text{ m} \\ 2\,0\,1\,4 \text{ m} \\ +\ 2\,9\,4\, \text{ m} \\ \hline 8\,5\,9\,8 \text{ m} \\ \hline \end{array} \qquad \begin{array}{r} 3\,0\,1\, \text{ m} \\ 3\,6\,8\,2 \text{ m} \\ +\ 3\,2\,4 \text{ m} \\ \hline 8\,2\,0\,7 \text{ m} \\ \hline \end{array} \qquad \begin{array}{r} 2\,4\,8\,5 \text{ m} \\ 1\,0\,0\,1 \text{ m} \\ +\ 8\,3\, \text{ m} \\ \hline 9\,3\,2\,4 \text{ m} \\ \hline \end{array}$$

Three travelling salespeople compare the distances they travel in a month. Mr Jones travels 4821 km, Mrs Patel travels 3146 km, and Mrs Ogilvy travels 2984 km.
How far do they travel altogether?

Subtracting 3- and 4-digit numbers

Work out the answer to each sum.

$$\begin{array}{r} {}^{2}\!\!\not{3}\,{}^{1}\!\!2\,65 \text{ m} \\ -\ 1\,344 \text{ m} \\ \hline 1\,921 \text{ m} \end{array}$$

$$\begin{array}{r} {}^{4}\!\!\not{5}\,{}^{1}\!\!2\,{}^{1}\!\!1\,{}^{1}\!\!6 \\ £5\,216 \\ -\ £2\,561 \\ \hline £2\,655 \end{array}$$

Work out the answer to each sum.

$$\begin{array}{r} 6\,314 \text{ m} \\ -\ 2\,402 \text{ m} \\ \hline \end{array}$$

$$\begin{array}{r} 8\,259 \text{ m} \\ -\ 3\,748 \text{ m} \\ \hline \end{array}$$

$$\begin{array}{r} 3\,144 \text{ m} \\ -\ 1\,622 \text{ m} \\ \hline \end{array}$$

$$\begin{array}{r} 7\,252 \text{ m} \\ -\ 4\,340 \text{ m} \\ \hline \end{array}$$

$$\begin{array}{r} £6\,324 \\ -\ £3\,521 \\ \hline \end{array}$$

$$\begin{array}{r} £8\,125 \\ -\ £2\,503 \\ \hline \end{array}$$

$$\begin{array}{r} £7\,423 \\ -\ £3\,500 \\ \hline \end{array}$$

$$\begin{array}{r} £2\,841 \\ -\ £1\,900 \\ \hline \end{array}$$

Write the answer in the box.

£4 536 − £1 602 =

£3 719 − £1 904 =

7 700 m − 4 800 m =

3 624 m − 1 814 m =

Work out the answer to each sum.

$$\begin{array}{r} 3\,213 \text{ m} \\ -\ 1\,715 \text{ m} \\ \hline \end{array}$$

$$\begin{array}{r} 8\,412 \text{ m} \\ -\ 4\,423 \text{ m} \\ \hline \end{array}$$

$$\begin{array}{r} 9\,634 \text{ m} \\ -\ 2\,746 \text{ m} \\ \hline \end{array}$$

$$\begin{array}{r} 5\,511 \text{ m} \\ -\ 1\,525 \text{ m} \\ \hline \end{array}$$

Put the missing numbers in these sums.

$$\begin{array}{r} £\,5\ \ \ \ 3\,7 \\ -£\,2\ \ 3\,4\,8 \\ \hline £\,3\ \ 0\,8 \end{array}$$

$$\begin{array}{r} £\ \ \ \ 9\,2\,3 \\ -£\,1\ \ 1\,4\,6 \\ \hline £\,3\,7\ \ 7 \end{array}$$

$$\begin{array}{r} 7\ 6\,3\,4 \text{ m} \\ -\ \ \ 5\,4\ \ \ \text{ m} \\ \hline 5\ 0\,9\,0 \text{ m} \end{array}$$

$$\begin{array}{r} 2\ 1\,5\,1 \text{ m} \\ -\ 1\ \ \ 4\,3 \text{ m} \\ \hline 3\,0\ \ \ \text{ m} \end{array}$$

A football stadium took £2 321 on Saturday. The week before they took £4 211. How much more did they take last week than this week?

13

Subtracting with 0 on top

Work out the answer to each sum.

$$
\begin{array}{r} {}^{4\,1}450 \\ -\ \ 27 \\ \hline 423 \end{array}
\qquad
\begin{array}{r} {}^{5\,3\,1}3\,640 \\ -\ \ 546 \\ \hline 3\,094 \end{array}
$$

Work out the answer to each sum.

$$
\begin{array}{r} 560 \\ -\ 26 \\ \hline \end{array}
\quad
\begin{array}{r} 390 \\ -\ 34 \\ \hline \end{array}
\quad
\begin{array}{r} 420 \\ -\ 16 \\ \hline \end{array}
\quad
\begin{array}{r} 330 \\ -\ 25 \\ \hline \end{array}
\quad
\begin{array}{r} 430 \\ -\ 114 \\ \hline \end{array}
$$

$$
\begin{array}{r} 720 \\ -\ 319 \\ \hline \end{array}
\quad
\begin{array}{r} 850 \\ -\ 526 \\ \hline \end{array}
\quad
\begin{array}{r} 680 \\ -\ 351 \\ \hline \end{array}
\quad
\begin{array}{r} 520 \\ -\ 134 \\ \hline \end{array}
\quad
\begin{array}{r} 940 \\ -\ 455 \\ \hline \end{array}
$$

$$
\begin{array}{r} 810 \\ -\ 247 \\ \hline \end{array}
\quad
\begin{array}{r} 730 \\ -\ 141 \\ \hline \end{array}
\quad
\begin{array}{r} 5\,230 \\ -\ 143 \\ \hline \end{array}
\quad
\begin{array}{r} 9\,520 \\ -\ 206 \\ \hline \end{array}
\quad
\begin{array}{r} 8\,140 \\ -\ 128 \\ \hline \end{array}
$$

$$
\begin{array}{r} 3\,630 \\ -\ 444 \\ \hline \end{array}
\quad
\begin{array}{r} 2\,370 \\ -\ 425 \\ \hline \end{array}
\quad
\begin{array}{r} 8\,730 \\ -\ 826 \\ \hline \end{array}
\quad
\begin{array}{r} 4\,210 \\ -\ 317 \\ \hline \end{array}
\quad
\begin{array}{r} 3\,580 \\ -\ 656 \\ \hline \end{array}
$$

$$
\begin{array}{r} 4\,360 \\ -\ 574 \\ \hline \end{array}
\quad
\begin{array}{r} 7\,210 \\ -\ 325 \\ \hline \end{array}
\quad
\begin{array}{r} 5\,480 \\ -\ 694 \\ \hline \end{array}
\quad
\begin{array}{r} 9\,670 \\ -\ 795 \\ \hline \end{array}
\quad
\begin{array}{r} 7\,210 \\ -\ 843 \\ \hline \end{array}
$$

$$
\begin{array}{r} 8\,540 \\ -\ 564 \\ \hline \end{array}
\quad
\begin{array}{r} 2\,640 \\ -\ 645 \\ \hline \end{array}
\quad
\begin{array}{r} 1\,110 \\ -\ 113 \\ \hline \end{array}
\quad
\begin{array}{r} 6\,340 \\ -2\,555 \\ \hline \end{array}
\quad
\begin{array}{r} 7\,230 \\ -\ 6\,452 \\ \hline \end{array}
$$

$$
\begin{array}{r} 5\,420 \\ -3\,434 \\ \hline \end{array}
\quad
\begin{array}{r} 7\,650 \\ -6\,998 \\ \hline \end{array}
\quad
\begin{array}{r} 9\,730 \\ -2\,843 \\ \hline \end{array}
\quad
\begin{array}{r} 6\,820 \\ -1\,752 \\ \hline \end{array}
\quad
\begin{array}{r} 3\,590 \\ -\ 1\,591 \\ \hline \end{array}
$$

Real life problems

Work out the answer to each sum.

A farmer's herd of cows produces 245 litres of milk. If he has 97 litres left, how much did he sell?

148 litres

```
  1 131
   245
 −  97
   148
```

A farmer has 97 litres of milk. His herd produces another 127 litres. How much does he now have?

224 litres

```
    97
 + 127
   224
   1 1
```

Work out the answer to each sum.

Sally buys 3 boxes of chocolates weighing 650 g, 575 g, and 345 g. What is the total weight of the chocolates?

A car has a full tank of 26.95 litres of petrol. If a journey uses up 12.47 litres, how much petrol will be left in the tank?

In a science experiment to test friction Frank is testing how far different model cars will roll down a ramp. Car A travels 95.47 cm, car B travels 83.32 cm, and car C travels 72.21 cm.

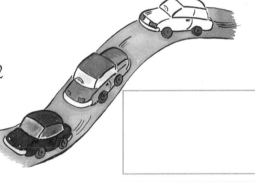

How much further does car A travel than car B?

How much further does car B travel than car C?

At the end of the experiment, what would the distance be between car A and car C?

What is the total distance travelled by the three cars?

Adding decimal fractions

Write the answer to each sum.

£5.22
+ £3.49

£4.34
+ £2.56

£8.21
+ £4.49

£3.28
+ £9.22

Write the answer to each sum.

2.77 m
+ 4.59 m

6.58 m
+ 3.54 m

7.37 m
+ 2.76 m

8.09 m
+ 4.96 m

Write the answer to each sum in the box.

£3.39 + £5.52 =

£6.37 + £5.09 =

£7.46 + £9.53 =

£8.22 + £1.19 =

3.77 m + 1.99 m =

5.24 m + 8.37 m =

Work out the answer to each sum.

Sandra has saved up £3.99. Her Mum gives her £1.62. How much does she now have?

Mrs Jones's car is 4.53 m long. Mr Jones's car is 5.24 m long. How long must their drive be in order to fit both cars in end to end?

16

Adding decimal fractions

Write the answer to each sum.

```
    £4.96              7.92 m
  + £2.83            + 1.68 m
  _____           _____
    £7.79              9.60 m
      1                 1  1
```

Write the answer to each sum.

```
    £8.94        £9.57        £7.96        £5.73
  + £5.88      + £9.99      + £4.78      + £9.97
  _____     _____     _____     _____


  _____     _____     _____     _____
```

```
    6.43 m       7.34 m       8.62 m       3.04 m
  + 8.57 m     + 9.99 m     + 8.08 m     + 5.76 m
  _____     _____     _____     _____


  _____     _____     _____     _____
```

Write the answer to each sum in the box.

£5.03 + £6.49 =   £2.74 + £9.61 =

£8.32 + £9.58 =   £1.29 + £4.83 =

5.26 m + 9.19 m =   2.04 m + 9.97 m =

Work out the answer to each sum.

Anna buys a can of drink for 45p and a sandwich for £1.39. How much does she pay?

Mr Bailey buys two wardrobes. One is 1.29 m wide and the other is 96 cm wide. How much space will they take up if they are put side by side?

Subtracting decimal fractions

Write the answer to each sum.

$$
\begin{array}{r}
{}^{7}\cancel{8}.{}^{1}\cancel{2}{}^{1}3 \\
\pounds 8.\overset{1}{2}3 \\
- \ \pounds 4.78 \\
\hline
\pounds 3.45 \\
\hline
\end{array}
\qquad\qquad
\begin{array}{r}
{}^{1}\ \ {}^{1}5\ {}^{1} \\
2.64 \ \text{m} \\
- \ 1.77 \ \text{m} \\
\hline
0.87 \ \text{m} \\
\hline
\end{array}
$$

Write the answer to each sum.

$$
\begin{array}{r}
\pounds 8.24 \\
- \ \pounds 5.36 \\
\hline
\end{array}
\qquad
\begin{array}{r}
\pounds 6.27 \\
- \ \pounds 3.48 \\
\hline
\end{array}
\qquad
\begin{array}{r}
\pounds 3.12 \\
- \ \pounds 1.23 \\
\hline
\end{array}
\qquad
\begin{array}{r}
\pounds 9.47 \\
- \ \pounds 4.79 \\
\hline
\end{array}
$$

Write the answer to each sum.

$$
\begin{array}{r}
5.21 \ \text{m} \\
- \ 2.99 \ \text{m} \\
\hline
\end{array}
\qquad
\begin{array}{r}
3.64 \ \text{m} \\
- \ 1.99 \ \text{m} \\
\hline
\end{array}
\qquad
\begin{array}{r}
9.12 \ \text{m} \\
- \ 3.99 \ \text{m} \\
\hline
\end{array}
\qquad
\begin{array}{r}
6.63 \ \text{m} \\
- \ 2.94 \ \text{m} \\
\hline
\end{array}
$$

Write the answer in the box.

£2.22 – £1.63 =   £8.14 – £3.25 =

£9.76 – £3.87 =   £5.71 – £1.92 =

7.71 m – 1.99 m =   3.55 m – 1.89 m =

Work out the answer to each sum.

Kofi's Mum gave him £5.75 to spend at the shops.
He came back with £1.87.
How much did he spend?

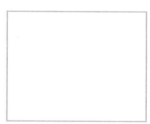

The end of Mrs Brophy's hosepipe was damaged.
The pipe was 4 m 32 cm long and she cut off 1 m 49 cm.
How much did she have left?

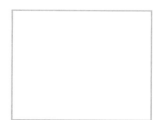

Subtracting decimal fractions

Write the answer to each sum.

$$
\begin{array}{r}
^{7}\!\!^{1}\!\!^{2}\!\!^{1} \\
£8.\cancel{3}1 \\
- £2.94 \\
\hline
£5.37
\end{array}
\qquad\qquad
\begin{array}{r}
^{5}\!\!^{1}\!\!^{1}\!\!^{1} \\
6.23 \text{ m} \\
- 2.84 \text{ m} \\
\hline
3.39 \text{ m}
\end{array}
$$

Work out the answer to each sum.

$$
\begin{array}{r} £5.31 \\ - \quad £1.89 \\ \hline \\ \hline \end{array}
\quad
\begin{array}{r} £8.24 \\ - \quad £2.87 \\ \hline \\ \hline \end{array}
\quad
\begin{array}{r} £7.23 \\ - \quad £3.44 \\ \hline \\ \hline \end{array}
\quad
\begin{array}{r} £6.23 \\ - \quad £1.24 \\ \hline \\ \hline \end{array}
\quad
\begin{array}{r} £4.11 \\ - \quad £1.12 \\ \hline \\ \hline \end{array}
$$

Write the answer to each sum.

$$
\begin{array}{r} 8.14 \text{ m} \\ - \quad 2.97 \text{ m} \\ \hline \\ \hline \end{array}
\quad
\begin{array}{r} 6.33 \text{ m} \\ - \quad 2.94 \text{ m} \\ \hline \\ \hline \end{array}
\quad
\begin{array}{r} 9.11 \text{ m} \\ - \quad 1.32 \text{ m} \\ \hline \\ \hline \end{array}
\quad
\begin{array}{r} 6.23 \text{ m} \\ - \quad 2.24 \text{ m} \\ \hline \\ \hline \end{array}
\quad
\begin{array}{r} 7.48 \text{ m} \\ - \quad 3.49 \text{ m} \\ \hline \\ \hline \end{array}
$$

Write the answer in the box.

£7.14 – £3.17 =   £3.39 – £1.47 =

£8.51 – £6.59 =   £6.23 – £5.34 =

8.14 m – 3.46 m =   7.42 m – 4.57 m =

Work out the answer to each sum.

Suzanne goes to the cinema with £5.13 to spend. She buys a hot dog for £2.49. How much does she have left?

Gita's garden is 7.43 m long. Josh's garden is 9.21 m long. How much longer is Josh's garden than Gita's?

Improper fractions

Convert the improper fraction $\frac{17}{10}$ to a mixed number. (Remember: an improper fraction has a numerator that is larger than the denominator.)

Mixed Number	Working out
$\frac{17}{10}$ $1\frac{7}{10}$	$\frac{17}{10} = \frac{10}{10}$ and $\frac{7}{10}$

Convert these improper fractions to mixed numbers.

	Mixed Number	Working out
$\frac{19}{10}$		
$\frac{15}{7}$		
$\frac{10}{3}$		
$\frac{23}{15}$		
$\frac{49}{8}$		
$\frac{51}{6}$		

Number lines

Write these fractions in the right places on the number line.

$$\frac{3}{4} \quad \frac{7}{10} \quad \frac{4}{5} \quad \frac{11}{20} \quad \frac{17}{20} \quad \frac{1}{2} \quad \frac{1}{4}$$

Write these fractions, improper fractions and mixed numbers in the right places on the number lines.

$$\frac{1}{3} \quad \frac{1}{2} \quad \frac{2}{10} \quad \frac{9}{10} \quad \frac{3}{5} \quad \frac{5}{6} \quad \frac{2}{3}$$

$$3\frac{1}{2} \quad 1\frac{2}{5} \quad 3\frac{1}{10} \quad \frac{49}{10} \quad \frac{9}{2} \quad 2\frac{3}{5}$$

$$\frac{15}{2} \quad 6\frac{2}{3} \quad \frac{77}{12} \quad 8\frac{1}{4} \quad 9\frac{3}{4} \quad \frac{28}{3}$$

Multiplying by units

Work out each answer.

456	823	755
x 6	x 8	x 9
2736	*6584*	*6795*

Work out each answer.

394	736	827	943
x 7	x 7	x 8	x 9

643	199	821	547
x 6	x 6	x 7	x 8

501	377	843	222
x 7	x 8	x 8	x 9

471	223	606	513
x 9	x 8	x 6	x 7

Work out each answer.

A crate holds 550 apples. How many apples will there be in 8 crates?

A swimming pool can hold a maximum of 760 people. What is the maximum number that can visit the pool in 5 sessions?

Dividing by units

Work out these division sums.

$$180\frac{1}{2}$$
$$2\overline{)361}$$

$$141\frac{1}{3}$$
$$3\overline{)424}$$

$$58\frac{3}{4}$$
$$4\overline{)235}$$

Work out these division sums. Part of the answer has been done for you.

$$2\overline{)413}^{\,2}$$

$$4\overline{)643}^{\,4}$$

$$3\overline{)572}^{\,3}$$

$$4\overline{)817}^{\,4}$$

$$2\overline{)203}^{\,2}$$

$$3\overline{)148}^{\,3}$$

$$4\overline{)951}^{\,4}$$

$$2\overline{)365}^{\,2}$$

$$3\overline{)200}^{\,3}$$

Now try these.

$$4\overline{)659}$$

$$2\overline{)265}$$

$$2\overline{)971}$$

$$4\overline{)737}$$

$$3\overline{)851}$$

$$4\overline{)203}$$

$$2\overline{)101}$$

$$5\overline{)754}$$

$$5\overline{)633}$$

Write the answer in the box.

What is 563 divided by 2?

Divide 293 by 5.

What is 374 divided by 3?

Divide 767 by 4.

Dividing by units

Work out these division sums.

$$62\frac{6}{9} = 62\frac{2}{3}$$

$$9\overline{\smash{)}564}$$

$$66\frac{1}{7}$$

$$7\overline{\smash{)}463}$$

Work out these division sums. Part of the answer has been done for you.

$$7\overline{\smash{)}403}^{\,7}$$

$$8\overline{\smash{)}655}^{\,8}$$

$$9\overline{\smash{)}205}^{\,9}$$

$$9\overline{\smash{)}745}^{\,9}$$

$$6\overline{\smash{)}637}^{\,6}$$

$$7\overline{\smash{)}323}^{\,7}$$

$$9\overline{\smash{)}574}^{\,9}$$

$$6\overline{\smash{)}431}^{\,6}$$

$$7\overline{\smash{)}121}^{\,7}$$

Now try these.

$$6\overline{\smash{)}527}$$

$$7\overline{\smash{)}599}$$

$$8\overline{\smash{)}300}$$

$$9\overline{\smash{)}217}$$

$$9\overline{\smash{)}404}$$

$$6\overline{\smash{)}777}$$

$$8\overline{\smash{)}630}$$

$$6\overline{\smash{)}423}$$

$$7\overline{\smash{)}859}$$

Write the answer in the box.

What is 759 divided by 7?

Divide 941 by 9.

What is 463 divided by 8?

Divide 232 by 6.

Real life problems

Work out the answer to each sum.

Jacob spent £4.68 at the shops and had £4.77 left. How much did he have to start with?

£9.45

```
   £4.77
+  £4.68
   £9.45
    1 1
```

Tracy receives £3.00 a week as pocket money. How much will she have if she saves it for 8 weeks?

£24.00

```
   £3.00
×      8
  £24.00
```

Work out the answer to each sum.

A cinema charges £4 for each ticket. If it sells 360 tickets for a performance, how much does it take?

David has saved £9.59. His sister has £3.24 less. How much does she have?

The cost for 9 children to go to a theme park is £72. How much does each child pay? If only 6 children go what will the cost be?

Paul has £3.69. He is given another £5.25 and goes out and buys a CD single for £3.99. How much does he have left?

Ian has £20 savings. He decides to spend $\frac{1}{4}$ of it. How much does he have left?

25

Real life problems

Work out the answer to each sum.

Nina has an hour to do her homework.
She needs to spend $\frac{1}{3}$ of her time on Maths.
How many minutes does she spend doing
her Maths?

20 minutes

1 hour is 60 minutes

$$3 \overline{)60} \quad 20$$

David makes 2 long jumps of 1.78 m and 2.19 m.
How far does he jump altogether?

3.97 m

$$\begin{array}{r} 1.78\,\text{m} \\ +\ 2.19\,\text{m} \\ \hline 3.97\,\text{m} \\ \scriptstyle 1 \end{array}$$

Work out the answer to each sum.

Moi has a can of lemonade
containing 400 ml. She drinks
$\frac{1}{4}$ of it. How much is left?

David runs 50 m in 8 seconds.
If he runs at the same speed for
the whole race how far does he
run in 1 second?

A large jar of coffee contains 1.75 kg
when full. If 1.48 kg is left in the jar,
how much has been used?

A worker can fill 145 packets of
tea in 15 minutes. How many
packets can he fill in 1 hour?

Jennifer's computer is 41.63 cm wide and
her printer is 48.37 cm wide. How much
space can she have between them if her
desk is 1.5 m wide?

Perimeters of squares and rectangles

Find the perimeter of this rectangle.
To find the perimeter of a rectangle
or a square we add the two lengths
and the two widths together.
e.g.   6 cm + 6 cm + 4 cm + 4 cm
= 20 cm
We can also do this by writing
(2 x 6) cm + (2 x 4) cm
= 12 cm + 8 cm = 20 cm

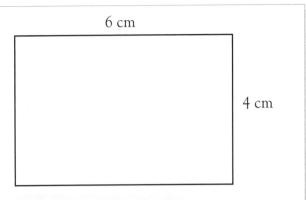

6 cm

4 cm

20 cm

Find the perimeters of these rectangles and squares.

4 cm

1 cm

_____ cm

3 cm

3 cm

_____ cm

2 cm

3 cm

_____ cm

3 cm

2 cm

_____ cm

1 cm

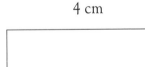

1 cm

_____ cm

4 cm

2 cm

_____ cm

4 cm

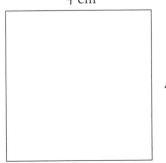

4 cm

_____ cm

4 cm

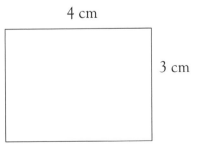

3 cm

_____ cm

2 cm

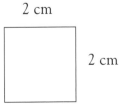

2 cm

_____ cm

Problems with time

Work out the answer to each sum.

Caitlin spends 35 minutes on her homework each day from Monday to Friday. How many minutes does she spend on her homework in one week?

175 min

Jenny spends 175 minutes on her homework Monday to Friday. How much time does she spend each day?

35 min

```
 35 min
  x 5
175 min
   2
```

```
      35 min
5 | 1 7⁵ 5
```

Work out the answer to each sum.

Amy works from 9 a.m. until 5 p.m. She has a lunch break from noon until 1 p.m. How many hours does she work in a 5 day week?

School children have 15 minutes' break time in the morning and 10 minutes' break time in the afternoon. How many minutes break time do they have in a week?

John takes 2 hours to do a job. If he shares the work with 3 of his friends, how long will it take?

Mr Tambo spends 7 days building a patio. If he worked a total of 56 hours and he spread the work evenly between the seven days, how long did he work each day?

Ben takes 44 hours building a remote-controlled aeroplane. If he spent 4 hours a day working on it:
How many days did it take?
How many hours per day would he have to work if he wanted to finish it in 6 days?

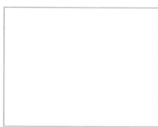

28

Converting units

Convert 25 centimetres to milimetres.   Convert 200p to pounds.

25 x 10 = 250 mm   200 ÷ 100 = £2

Convert these centimetres to millimetres.

40 cm		15 cm		9 cm	
12 cm		34 cm		62 cm	
43 cm		96 cm		105 cm	
92 cm		20 cm		426 cm	

Convert these millimetres to centimetres.

30 mm		100 mm		120 mm	
60 mm		90 mm		200 mm	
130 mm		10 mm		400 mm	

Convert these pounds to pence.

£35		£600		£15	
£12		£36		£95	
£72		£4		£250	

Convert these pence to pounds.

450p		900p		6000p	
250p		400p		150p	
100p		300p		750p	

Converting units

Convert 300 centimetres to metres.   Convert 4 kilometres to metres.

$300 \div 100 = 3$ m $4 \times 1000 = 4000$ m

Convert these centimetres to metres.

500 cm	900 cm	400 cm
8 000 cm	3 000 cm	4 000 cm
9 800 cm	8 300 cm	6 200 cm
36 800 cm	94 200 cm	73 500 cm

Convert these metres to centimetres.

47 m	29 m	84 m
69 m	24 m	38 m
146 m	237 m	921 m

Convert these metres to kilometres.

5 000 m	6 000 m	9 000 m
15 000 m	27 000 m	71 000 m
19 000 m	86 000 m	42 000 m

Convert these kilometres to metres.

7 km	9 km	4 km
23 km	46 km	87 km
12 km	96 km	39 km

Frequency table with grouped data

20 children score runs in a cricket match. Here is a list of their scores:
12, 3, 3, 14, 7, 9, 19, 10, 8, 16, 8, 20, 17, 8, 7, 16, 13, 5, 12, 19.
Draw the frequency table and group this data.

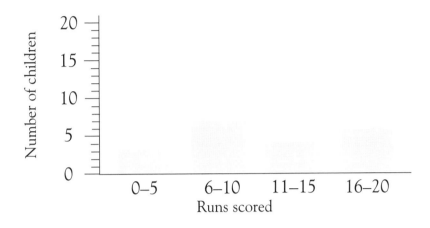

A class of 50 children did a science test. Here are their results:
5, 16, 6, 12, 2, 17, 19, 14, 18, 20, 18, 6, 5, 5, 4, 7, 8, 16, 9, 3,
12, 2, 14, 18, 14, 19, 4, 7, 3, 4, 20, 18, 20, 15, 20, 16, 16, 8, 15,
11, 9, 12, 16, 7, 17, 6, 9, 15, 18, 20.

Draw a frequency table to show this data.

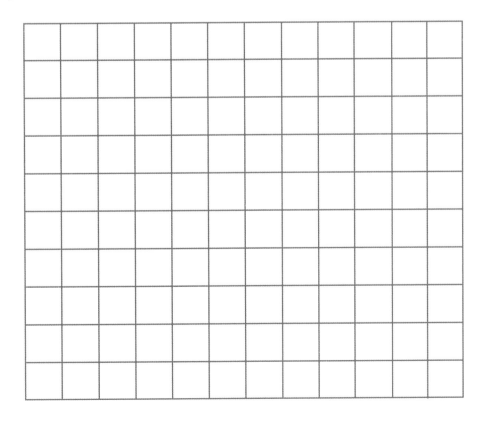

Rotational symmetry

What is the order of rotation of this shape?

The order of rotation is   6

This shape has an order of rotation of 6 because it can be turned onto itself 6 times.

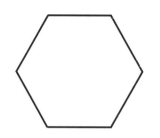

What is the order of rotation of these shapes?

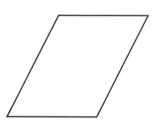

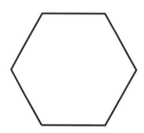

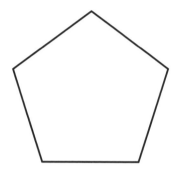

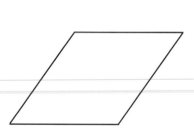

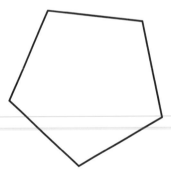

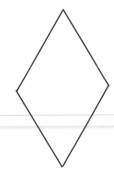

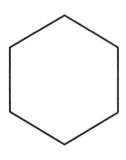

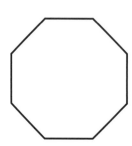

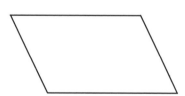

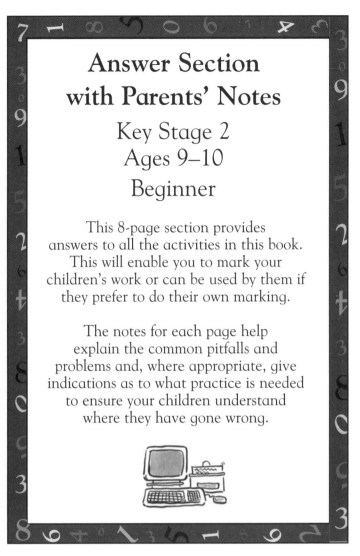

Answer Section with Parents' Notes

Key Stage 2
Ages 9–10
Beginner

This 8-page section provides answers to all the activities in this book. This will enable you to mark your children's work or can be used by them if they prefer to do their own marking.

The notes for each page help explain the common pitfalls and problems and, where appropriate, give indications as to what practice is needed to ensure your children understand where they have gone wrong.

---

2 ⭐ Partition numbers to 10 000 000

| How many hundreds are the same as 7000? | 70 | hundreds (70 x 100 = 7 000) |
| What is the nine worth in 694? | 90 | (because the nine digit is in the 10s column) |

How many tens are the same as:

400	40	tens	600	60	tens	900	90	tens
200	20	tens	1 300	130	tens	4 700	470	tens
4 800	480	tens	1 240	124	tens	1 320	132	tens
2 630	263	tens	5 920	592	tens	4 350	435	tens

What is the 7 worth in these numbers?

| 76 | 70 | | 720 | 700 | | 137 | 7 |
| 7 122 | 7 000 | | 74 301 | 70 000 | | 724 | 700 |

What is the 3 worth in these numbers?

| 324 126 | 300 000 | | 3 927 141 | 3 000 000 | | 214 623 | 3 |
| 8 254 320 | 300 | | 3 711 999 | 3 000 000 | | 124 372 | 300 |

How many hundreds are the same as:

6 400	64	hundreds	8 500	85	hundreds
19 900	199	hundreds	36 200	362	hundreds
524 600	5 246	hundreds	712 400	7 124	hundreds

What is the 8 worth in these numbers?

| 8 214 631 | 8 000 000 | | 2 398 147 | 8 000 | | 463 846 | 800 |
| 287 034 | 80 000 | | 8 110 927 | 8 000 000 | | 105 428 | 8 |

Explain to children that in the number 400, if you put the 4 into the tens column you have 40 tens. With 4 800 if you put the 4 and the 8 into the tens column you have 480 tens. This could be done with lots of different numbers until the children are confident.

---

3 Multiplying and dividing by 10 ⭐

Write the answer in the box.

$37 \times 10 = $ 370 $58 \div 10 = $ 5.8

Write the answer in the box.

$94 \times 10 = $ 940	$13 \times 10 = $ 130	$37 \times 10 = $ 370
$36 \times 10 = $ 360	$47 \times 10 = $ 470	$54 \times 10 = $ 540
$236 \times 10 = $ 2 360	$419 \times 10 = $ 4 190	$262 \times 10 = $ 2 620
$531 \times 10 = $ 5 310	$674 \times 10 = $ 6 740	$801 \times 10 = $ 8 010

Write the answer in the box.

$92 \div 10 = $ 9.2	$48 \div 10 = $ 4.8	$37 \div 10 = $ 3.7
$18 \div 10 = $ 1.8	$29 \div 10 = $ 2.9	$54 \div 10 = $ 5.4
$345 \div 10 = $ 34.5	$354 \div 10 = $ 35.4	$723 \div 10 = $ 72.3
$531 \div 10 = $ 53.1	$262 \div 10 = $ 26.2	$419 \div 10 = $ 41.9

Find the number that has been multiplied by 10.

23 $\times 10 = 230$	75 $\times 10 = 750$	99 $\times 10 = 990$
48 $\times 10 = 480$	13 $\times 10 = 130$	25 $\times 10 = 250$
52 $\times 10 = 520$	39 $\times 10 = 390$	27 $\times 10 = 270$
62 $\times 10 = 620$	86 $\times 10 = 860$	17 $\times 10 = 170$

Find the number that has been divided by 10.

47 $\div 10 = 4.7$	68 $\div 10 = 6.8$	124 $\div 10 = 12.4$
257 $\div 10 = 25.7$	362 $\div 10 = 36.2$	314 $\div 10 = 31.4$
408 $\div 10 = 40.8$	672 $\div 10 = 67.2$	809 $\div 10 = 80.9$
924 $\div 10 = 92.4$	327 $\div 10 = 32.7$	563 $\div 10 = 56.3$

Children should realise that multiplying a number by 10 is the same as adding a 0 to the original figure. When dividing by 10 explain how the number moves one place to the right. In the last two sections, the inverse operation gives the number that begins the sum.

---

4 ⭐ Ordering sets of amounts

Write these amounts in order, starting with the smallest.

| 3 100 km | 24 km | 1 821 km | 247 km | 4 km | 960 km |
| 4 km | 24 km | 247 km | 960 km | 1 821 km | 3 100 km |

Write these amounts in order, starting with the smallest.

£526	£15 940	£1 504	£826	£37 532
£526	£826	£1 504	£15 940	£37 532
720 m	7 200 m	27 410 m	15 m	247 m
15 m	247 m	720 m	7 200 m	27 410 m
70 000 l	650 l	26 000 l	6 500 l	7 000 l
650 l	6 500 l	7 000 l	26 000 l	70 000 l
656 kg	9 565 kg	22 942 kg	752 247 kg	1 327 kg
656 kg	1 327 kg	9 565 kg	22 942 kg	752 247 kg
9 520 yrs	320 yrs	4 681 yrs	8 940 yrs	20 316 yrs
320 yrs	4 681 yrs	8 940 yrs	9 520 yrs	20 316 yrs
217 846 kg	75 126 kg	8 940 kg	14 632 kg	175 kg
175 kg	8 940 kg	14 632 kg	75 126 kg	217 846 kg
9 420 km	764 km	25 811 km	114 243 km	7 240 km
764 km	7 240 km	9 420 km	25 811 km	114 243 km
£37 227	£1 365 240	£143 820	£950	£4 212
£950	£4 212	£37 227	£143 820	£1 365 240
24 091 m	59 473 m	1 237 m	426 m	837 201 m
426 m	1 237 m	24 091 m	59 473 m	837 201 m
47 632 kg	847 kg	9 625 kg	103 427 kg	2 330 kg
847 kg	2 330 kg	9 625 kg	47 632 kg	103 427 kg
7 340 m	249 m	12 746 m	32 m	17 407 321 m
32 m	249 m	7 340 m	12 746 m	17 407 321 m

If children are weak on place value help them to identify the significant digit when sorting the numbers. The most likely errors will be in the groups of numbers where the same digits have been used with different place values. Children may need to be alerted to this.

5 — Ordering sets with negative numbers

Write these numbers in order, starting with the smallest.

6	9	−3	5	−2	0

| −3 | −2 | 0 | 5 | 6 | 9 |

Put these numbers on the number line.

1   2   −1   −3   3   −4

−4 −3 −2 −1   0   1   2   3   4   5

Write these numbers in order, starting with the smallest.

7	3	−4	−1	6
−4	−1	3	6	7

4	−2	0	9	−5
−5	−2	0	4	9

10	3	−8	−7	9
−8	−7	3	9	10

−12	8	4	−2	−1
−12	−2	−1	4	8

11	−7	3	−2	0
−7	−2	0	3	11

12	8	−2	−8	6
−8	−2	6	8	12

Do the same with these groups of numbers.

4	7	−3	−1	9	−4	1	−8	0	2
−8	−4	−3	−1	0	1	2	4	7	9

2	−8	0	5	−14	20	−18	7	−5	10
−18	−14	−8	−5	0	2	5	7	10	20

5	−3	0	−7	−1	11	−15	2	9	−4
−15	−7	−4	−3	−1	0	2	5	9	11

−12	3	−7	8	25	−2	14	−9	12	−20
−20	−12	−9	−7	−2	3	8	12	14	25

Children may place the negative numbers out of sequence. Often −20 will be placed as a higher number than −18, because it looks bigger.

6 — Counting in constant steps

Continue each row.

Steps of 6	−5	1	7	13	19	25	31
Steps of 3	7	4	1	−2	−5	−8	−11

Continue each row.

−20	−10	0	10	20	30	40
−15	−10	−5	0	5	10	15
−9	−7	−5	−3	−1	1	3
−2	5	12	19	26	33	40
−11	−8	−5	−2	1	4	7
−2	6	14	22	30	38	46

Continue each row.

24	18	12	6	0	−6	−12
13	9	5	1	−3	−7	−11
7	3	−1	−5	−9	−13	−17
32	24	16	8	0	−8	−16
35	28	21	14	7	0	−7
8	5	2	−1	−4	−7	−10

Continue each row.

22	16	10	4	−2	−8	−14
−4	5	14	23	32	41	50
3	−2	−7	−12	−17	−22	−27
17	10	3	−4	−11	−18	−25
−1	2	5	8	11	14	17

It may be necessary to point out that the steps can be found by taking the first number away from the second. Encourage double-checking by taking the second from the third. Use terms such as 'difference' so children identify it with the word subtraction.

7 — Recognising multiples

Circle the multiples of 10.

14   (20)   25   (30)   47   (60)

Circle the multiples of 6.

20	(48)	56	(72)	25	35
1	3	(6)	16	26	(36)

Circle the multiples of 7.

(14)	24	(35)	27	47	(49)
(63)	(42)	52	37	64	71

Circle the multiples of 8.

25	31	(48)	84	(32)	(8)
18	54	(64)	35	(72)	28

Circle the multiples of 9.

17	(81)	(27)	35	92	106
(45)	53	(108)	(90)	33	95
64	(9)	28	(18)	(36)	98

Circle the multiples of 10.

15	35	(20)	46	(90)	(100)
44	37	(30)	29	(50)	45

Circle the multiples of 11.

24	(110)	123	54	(66)	90
45	(33)	87	98	(99)	(121)
43	(44)	65	(55)	21	(22)

Circle the multiples of 12.

136	134	(144)	109	(108)	(132)
(24)	34	58	68	(48)	(60)
35	29	(72)	74	(84)	94

Success on this page will basically depend on a knowledge of multiplication tables. Where children experience difficulty, it may be necessary to reinforce multiplication tables.

8 — Factors of numbers from 31 to 65

The factors of 40 are   1   2   4   5   8   10   20   40

Circle the factors of 56.

(1) (2) 3 (4) 5 6 (7) (8) (14) (28) 32 (56)

Find all the factors of these numbers.

The factors of 31 are	1, 31
The factors of 47 are	1, 47
The factors of 60 are	1, 2, 3, 4, 5, 6, 10, 12, 15, 20, 30, 60
The factors of 50 are	1, 2, 5, 10, 25, 50
The factors of 42 are	1, 2, 3, 6, 7, 14, 21, 42
The factors of 32 are	1, 2, 4, 8, 16, 32
The factors of 48 are	1, 2, 3, 4, 6, 8, 12, 16, 24, 48
The factors of 35 are	1, 5, 7, 35
The factors of 52 are	1, 2, 4, 13, 26, 52

Circle the factors of these numbers.

Which numbers are factors of 39?
(1) 2 (3) 4 5 8 9 10 (13) 14 15 20 25 (39)

Which numbers are factors of 45?
(1) (3) 4 (5) 8 (9) 12 (15) 16 21 24 36 40 44 (45)

Which numbers are factors of 61?
(1) 3 4 5 6 10 15 16 18 20 26 31 40 (61)

Which numbers are factors of 65?
(1) 2 4 (5) 6 8 9 10 12 (13) 14 15 30 60 (65)

Some numbers only have factors of 1 and themselves. They are called prime numbers. Write all the prime numbers between 31 and 65 in the box.

31, 37, 41, 43, 47, 53, 59, 61

Quite often some factors of numbers get missed. This becomes more likely as the numbers get larger. Encourage a systematic method of finding the factors. Children often forget that 1 and itself are factors of a number. Also discuss prime numbers with them.

Square numbers

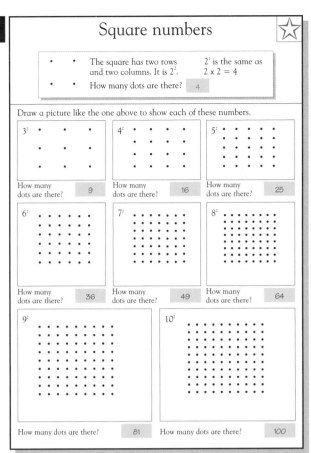

The square has two rows and two columns. It is 2^2. 2^2 is the same as $2 \times 2 = 4$

How many dots are there? 4

Draw a picture like the one above to show each of these numbers.

3^2 How many dots are there? 9

4^2 How many dots are there? 16

5^2 How many dots are there? 25

6^2 How many dots are there? 36

7^2 How many dots are there? 49

8^2 How many dots are there? 64

9^2 How many dots are there? 81

10^2 How many dots are there? 100

This is a traditional way of showing square numbers but many children will pick up the idea of 'multiplying the number by itself' fairly quickly. If the children pick up the idea do not make them draw the dots but talk through the work with them instead.

Finding fractions of amounts

Find $\frac{1}{2}$ of £25.00.

£25.00 ÷ 2 = £12.50   Remember that £12.5 is not correct.

Find $\frac{1}{10}$ of 3 cm.

3 cm ÷ 10 = 0.3 cm   or   30 mm ÷ 10 = 3 mm

0.3 cm is the same as 3 mm.

Find $\frac{1}{2}$ of these amounts.

24 cm	12 cm	30p	15p
£1.50	75 p	16 cm	8 cm
14 hours	7 hours	60 kg	30 kg

Find $\frac{1}{4}$ of these amounts.

20 min	5 min	16 l	4 l
8 km	2 km	36 hours	9 hours
48 g	12 g	24 cm	6 cm

Find $\frac{1}{10}$ of these amounts.

5 cm	0.5 cm	12 cm	1.2 cm
£4.00	40p	5 l	0.5 l
30p	3p	9 kg	0.9 kg
5 hours	0.5 hours	6 km	0.6 km

Find $\frac{1}{100}$ of these amounts.

£40.00	40p	50 cm	0.5 cm
20 km	0.2 km	90 g	0.9 g
50 m	0.5 m	36 l	0.36 l
15 hours	0.15 hours	£75.00	75p

If children find the 3rd section difficult, refer them back to page 3 for division by 10. You may need to explain that dividing by 100 means moving the number two places to the right. Children may write answers as decimals, e.g. 0.5 cm, or change the units, e.g. 5 mm.

Changing simple fractions and decimals

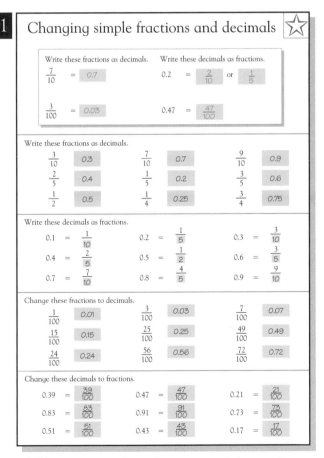

Write these fractions as decimals.

$\frac{7}{10}$ = 0.7

$\frac{3}{100}$ = 0.03

Write these decimals as fractions.

0.2 = $\frac{2}{10}$ or $\frac{1}{5}$

0.47 = $\frac{47}{100}$

Write these fractions as decimals.

$\frac{3}{10}$ = 0.3 $\frac{7}{10}$ = 0.7 $\frac{9}{10}$ = 0.9

$\frac{2}{5}$ = 0.4 $\frac{1}{5}$ = 0.2 $\frac{3}{5}$ = 0.6

$\frac{1}{2}$ = 0.5 $\frac{1}{4}$ = 0.25 $\frac{3}{4}$ = 0.75

Write these decimals as fractions.

0.1 = $\frac{1}{10}$ 0.2 = $\frac{1}{5}$ 0.3 = $\frac{3}{10}$

0.4 = $\frac{2}{5}$ 0.5 = $\frac{1}{2}$ 0.6 = $\frac{3}{5}$

0.7 = $\frac{7}{10}$ 0.8 = $\frac{4}{5}$ 0.9 = $\frac{9}{10}$

Change these fractions to decimals.

$\frac{1}{100}$ = 0.01 $\frac{3}{100}$ = 0.03 $\frac{7}{100}$ = 0.07

$\frac{15}{100}$ = 0.15 $\frac{25}{100}$ = 0.25 $\frac{49}{100}$ = 0.49

$\frac{24}{100}$ = 0.24 $\frac{56}{100}$ = 0.56 $\frac{72}{100}$ = 0.72

Change these decimals to fractions.

0.39 = $\frac{39}{100}$ 0.47 = $\frac{47}{100}$ 0.21 = $\frac{21}{100}$

0.83 = $\frac{83}{100}$ 0.91 = $\frac{91}{100}$ 0.73 = $\frac{73}{100}$

0.51 = $\frac{51}{100}$ 0.43 = $\frac{43}{100}$ 0.17 = $\frac{17}{100}$

Children may need reinforcement of place value in decimals. You may need to point out that $\frac{3}{10}$ is the same as 3 divided by 10, and that $\frac{15}{100}$ is the same as 15 divided by 100.

Adding two or three numbers

Work out the answer to each sum.

```
  5241 km
+ 3527 km
  8768 km
```
Remember to carry if you need to.

```
  2682 m
  3220 m
+ 2314 m
  8216 m
     1 1
```

Work out the answer to each sum.

```
  1985 km       5763 km       6247 km
+ 2841 km     + 3528 km     + 1519 km
  4826 km       9291 km       7766 km
```

```
  2640 km       3521 km       4813 km
  1739 km       2195 km       2000 km
+ 2101 km     + 2325 km     + 3458 km
  6480 km       8041 km      10271 km
```

Write the answer in the box.

2753 m + 1375 m = 4128 m   4813 m + 2427 m + 1023 m = 8263 m

3714 m + 5918 m = 9632 m   2349 m + 1773 m + 3859 m = 7981 m

Put the missing numbers in these sums.

```
  3642 m        1301 m        2485 m
  2014 m        3682 m        1001 m
+ 2942 m      + 3224 m      + 5838 m
  8598 m        8207 m        9324 m
```

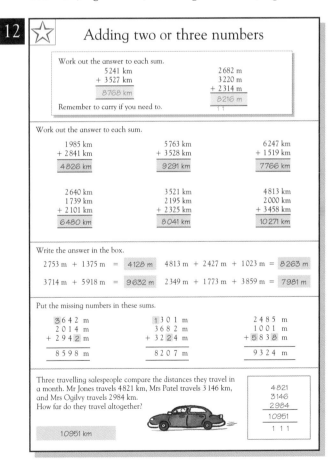

Three travelling salespeople compare the distances they travel in a month. Mr Jones travels 4821 km, Mrs Patel travels 3146 km, and Mrs Ogilvy travels 2984 km. How far do they travel altogether?

```
  4821
  3146
  2984
 10951
  1 1 1
```

10951 km

Sums on this page are similar to the previous page but with larger numbers. As the numbers get larger it is likely that children might make errors in carrying. Watch out for confusion when adding horizontally.

Subtracting 3- and 4-digit numbers ☆

Work out the answer to each sum.

$$\begin{array}{r} {}^{2}^{1}\\ \cancel{3}\,265 \text{ m}\\ -\ 1\,344 \text{ m}\\ \hline 1\,921 \text{ m} \end{array} \qquad \begin{array}{r} {}^{4}^{1}{}^{1}{}^{1}\\ \cancel{£5}\,216\\ -\ £2\,561\\ \hline £2\,655 \end{array}$$

Work out the answer to each sum.

6 314 m − 2 402 m **3 912 m**	8 259 m − 3 748 m **4 511 m**	3 144 m − 1 622 m **1 522 m**	7 252 m − 4 340 m **2 912 m**
£6 324 − £3 521 **£2 803**	£8 125 − £2 503 **£5 622**	£7 423 − £3 500 **£3 923**	£2 841 − £1 900 **£941**

Write the answer in the box.

£4 536 − £1 602 = **£2 934**   £3 719 − £1 904 = **£1 815**

7 700 m − 4 800 m = **2 900 m**   3 624 m − 1 814 m = **1 810 m**

Work out the answer to each sum.

3 213 m − 1 715 m **1 498 m**	8 412 m − 4 423 m **3 989 m**	9 634 m − 2 746 m **6 888 m**	5 511 m − 1 525 m **3 986 m**

Put the missing numbers in these sums.

£ 5 **4** 3 7 −£ 2 3 4 8 **£ 3 0 8 9**	£ 4 9 2 3 −£ 1 1 4 6 **£ 3 7 7 7**	7 6 3 4 m −2 5 **4** 4 m **5 0 9 0 m**	2 1 5 1 m −1 8 4 3 m **3 0 8 m**

A football stadium took £2 321 on Saturday. The week before they took £4 211. How much more did they take last week than this week?

$$\begin{array}{r} {}^{3}^{11}^{1}\\ \cancel{4}\,211\\ -\ 2\,321\\ \hline 1\,890 \end{array}$$

£1 890

The work on this page is similar to the previous page but decomposition is also required for the hundreds digits to be subtracted. This means 'borrowing' or 'stealing' from the digit on the left. It is better to use the term 'stealing' since the number is never returned.

☆ Subtracting with 0 on top

Work out the answer to each sum.

$$\begin{array}{r} {}^{4}{}^{1}\\ \cancel{4}\cancel{5}0\\ -\ 27\\ \hline 423 \end{array} \qquad \begin{array}{r} {}^{5}{}^{13}\\ 3\,\cancel{6}\cancel{4}0\\ -\ 546\\ \hline 3\,094 \end{array}$$

Work out the answer to each sum.

560 − 26 **534**	390 − 34 **356**	420 − 16 **404**	330 − 25 **305**	430 − 114 **316**
720 − 319 **401**	850 − 526 **324**	680 − 351 **329**	520 − 134 **386**	940 − 455 **485**
810 − 247 **563**	730 − 141 **589**	5 230 − 143 **5087**	9 520 − 206 **9314**	8 140 − 128 **8012**
3 630 − 444 **3186**	2 370 − 425 **1945**	8 730 − 826 **7904**	4 210 − 317 **3893**	3 580 − 656 **2924**
4 360 − 574 **3786**	7 210 − 325 **6885**	5 480 − 694 **4786**	9 670 − 795 **8875**	7 210 − 843 **6367**
8 540 − 564 **7976**	2 640 − 645 **1995**	1 110 − 113 **997**	6 340 −2 555 **3785**	7 230 − 6 452 **778**
5 420 −3 434 **1986**	7 650 −6 998 **652**	9 730 −2 843 **6887**	6 820 −1 752 **5068**	3 590 − 1 591 **1999**

This page is similar to the previous two, but the numbe[r] on top has a nought in the units column. If children h[ave] difficulty, explain that when 'stealing' a digit from the tens column, it goes together with the zero in the units column to make a ten.

Real life problems ☆

Work out the answer to each sum.

A farmer's herd of cows produces 245 litres of milk. If he has 97 litres left, how much did he sell?

148 litres

$$\begin{array}{r} {}^{1}{}^{3}{}^{1}\\ 2\cancel{4}\cancel{5}\\ -\ 97\\ \hline 148 \end{array}$$

A farmer has 97 litres of milk. His herd produces another 127 litres. How much does he now have?

224 litres

$$\begin{array}{r} 97\\ +\ 127\\ \hline 224\\ {}^{1}{}^{1} \end{array}$$

Work out the answer to each sum.

Sally buys 3 boxes of chocolates weighing 650 g, 575 g, and 345 g. What is the total weight of the chocolates?

1570 g (1.57 kg)

$$\begin{array}{r} 650\\ +\ 575\\ 345\\ \hline 1570\\ {}^{1}{}^{1} \end{array}$$

A car has a full tank of 26.95 litres of petrol. If a journey uses up 12.47 litres, how much petrol will be left in the tank?

14.48 litres

$$\begin{array}{r} {}^{8}{}^{1}\\ 26.\cancel{9}5\\ -\ 12.47\\ \hline 14.48 \end{array}$$

In a science experiment to test friction Frank is testing how far different model cars will roll down a ramp. Car A travels 95.47 cm, car B travels 83.32 cm, and car C travels 72.21 cm.

How much further does car A travel than car B?

12.15 cm

$$\begin{array}{r} 95.47\\ -\ 83.32\\ \hline 12.15 \end{array}$$

How much further does car B travel than car C?

11.11 cm

$$\begin{array}{r} 83.32\\ -\ 72.21\\ \hline 11.11 \end{array}$$

At the end of the experiment, what would the distance be between car A and car C?

23.26 cm

$$\begin{array}{r} 95.47\\ -\ 72.21\\ \hline 23.26 \end{array}$$

What is the total distance travelled by the three cars?

251 cm (2.51 m)

$$\begin{array}{r} 95.47\\ +83.32\\ 72.21\\ \hline 251.00\\ {}^{1}{}^{1}{}^{1} \end{array}$$

On this page, children can apply skills of addition and subtraction to real life problems, using various units of measurement. If they are unsure which operation to use, discuss whether the answer will be larger (addition) or smaller (subtraction).

☆ Adding decimal fractions

Write the answer to each sum.

£7.49 + £1.36 **£8.85** 1	4.18 m + 5.59 m **9.77 m** 1

Write the answer to each sum.

£5.22 + £3.49 **£8.71**	£4.34 + £2.56 **£6.90**	£8.21 + £4.49 **£12.70**	£3.28 + £9.22 **£12.50**

Write the answer to each sum.

2.77 m + 4.59 m **7.36 m**	6.58 m + 3.54 m **10.12 m**	7.37 m + 2.76 m **10.13 m**	8.09 m + 4.96 m **13.05 m**

Write the answer to each sum in the box.

£3.39 + £5.52 = **£8.91**   £6.37 + £5.09 = **£11.46**

£7.46 + £9.53 = **£16.99**   £8.22 + £1.19 = **£9.41**

3.77 m + 1.99 m = **5.76 m**   5.24 m + 8.37 m = **13.61 m**

Work out the answer to each sum.

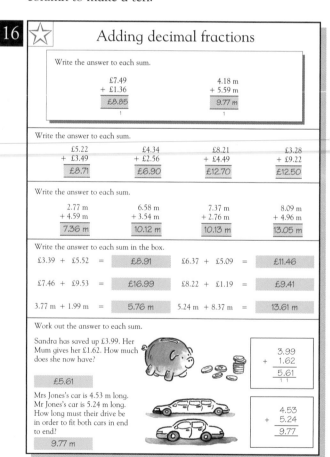

Sandra has saved up £3.99. Her Mum gives her £1.62. How much does she now have?

£5.61

$$\begin{array}{r} 3.99\\ +\ 1.62\\ \hline 5.61\\ {}^{1}{}^{1} \end{array}$$

Mrs Jones's car is 4.53 m long. Mr Jones's car is 5.24 m long. How long must their drive be in order to fit both cars in end to end?

9.77 m

$$\begin{array}{r} 4.53\\ +\ 5.24\\ \hline 9.77 \end{array}$$

This page should follow on from the earlier addition work. The most likely error will be misplacing the decimal point when adding horizontally. Less confident children may need to be reassured when carrying across the decimal point.

17 Adding decimal fractions ☆

Write the answer to each sum.

£4.96 + £2.83 **£7.79** ₁	7.92 m + 1.68 m **9.60 m** _{1 1}

Write the answer to each sum.

£8.94 + £5.88 **£14.82**	£9.57 + £9.99 **£19.56**	£7.96 + £4.78 **£12.74**	£5.73 + £9.97 **£15.70**
6.43 m + 8.57 m **15.00 m**	7.34 m + 9.99 m **17.33 m**	8.62 m + 8.08 m **16.70 m**	3.04 m + 5.76 m **8.80 m**

Write the answer to each sum in the box.

£5.03 + £6.49 = **£11.52**   £2.74 + £9.61 = **£12.35**

£8.32 + £9.58 = **£17.90**   £1.29 + £4.83 = **£6.12**

5.26 m +   9.19 m = **14.45 m**   2.04 m +   9.97 m = **12.01 m**

Work out the answer to each sum.

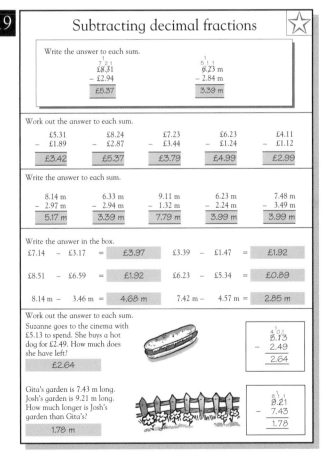

Anna buys a can of drink for 45p and a sandwich for £1.39. How much does she pay?
£1.84

| 1.39
+ 0.45
1.84
₁ |

Mr Bailey buys two wardrobes. One is 1.29 m wide and the other is 96 cm wide. How much space will they take up if they are put side by side?
2.25 m

| 1.29
+ 0.96
2.25
_{1 1} |

As with the previous page, the most likely errors will occur in positioning the decimal point in the horizontal sums. In the last section, explain to the children that 45p and 96 cm can be written as £0.45 and 0.96 m for the purposes of addition.

---

18 ☆ Subtracting decimal fractions

Write the answer to each sum.

_{7 1 1} £8.23 – £4.78 **£3.45**	_{1 5 1} 2.64 m – 1.77 m **0.87 m**

Write the answer to each sum.

£8.24 – £5.36 **£2.88**	£6.27 – £3.48 **£2.79**	£3.12 – £1.23 **£1.89**	£9.47 – £4.79 **£4.68**
5.21 m – 2.99 m **2.22 m**	3.64 m – 1.99 m **1.65 m**	9.12 m – 3.99 m **5.13 m**	6.63 m – 2.94 m **3.69m**

Write the answer in the box.

£2.22 – £1.63 = **£0.59**   £8.14 – £3.25 = **£4.89**

£9.76 – £3.87 = **£5.89**   £5.71 – £1.92 = **£3.79**

7.71 m –   1.99 m = **5.72 m**   3.55 m –   1.89 m = **1.66 m**

Work out the answer to each sum.

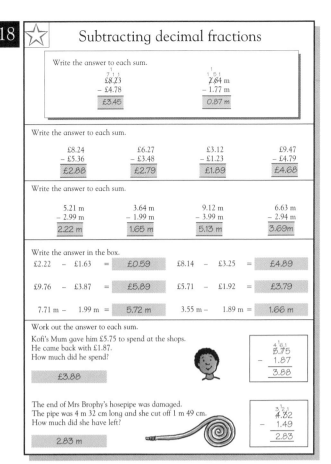

Kofi's Mum gave him £5.75 to spend at the shops. He came back with £1.87. How much did he spend?
£3.88

| _{4 16 1}
5.75
– 1.87
3.88 |

The end of Mrs Brophy's hosepipe was damaged. The pipe was 4 m 32 cm long and she cut off 1 m 49 cm. How much did she have left?
2.83 m

| _{3 12 1}
4.32
– 1.49
2.83 |

If the children are unsure, explain that once the decimal point is placed in the answer box the sum can be done as a conventional subtraction. Children may need to be reassured that they can steal across the decimal point.

---

19 Subtracting decimal fractions ☆

Write the answer to each sum.

_{7 2 1} £8.31 – £2.94 **£5.37**	_{5 1 1} 6.23 m – 2.84 m **3.39 m**

Work out the answer to each sum.

£5.31 – £1.89 **£3.42**	£8.24 – £2.87 **£5.37**	£7.23 – £3.44 **£3.79**	£6.23 – £1.24 **£4.99**	£4.11 – £1.12 **£2.99**

Write the answer to each sum.

8.14 m – 2.97 m **5.17 m**	6.33 m – 2.94 m **3.39 m**	9.11 m – 1.32 m **7.79 m**	6.23 m – 2.24 m **3.99 m**	7.48 m – 3.49 m **3.99 m**

Write the answer in the box.

£7.14 – £3.17 = **£3.97**   £3.39 – £1.47 = **£1.92**

£8.51 – £6.59 = **£1.92**   £6.23 – £5.34 = **£0.89**

8.14 m –   3.46 m = **4.68 m**   7.42 m –   4.57 m = **2.85 m**

Work out the answer to each sum.

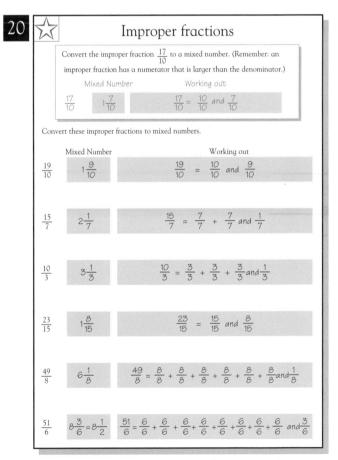

Suzanne goes to the cinema with £5.13 to spend. She buys a hot dog for £2.49. How much does she have left?
£2.64

| _{4 10 1}
5.13
– 2.49
2.64 |

Gita's garden is 7.43 m long. Josh's garden is 9.21 m long. How much longer is Josh's garden than Gita's?
1.78 m

| _{8 1 1}
9.21
– 7.43
1.78 |

This page involves more practice of the work done on the previous page.

---

20 ☆ Improper fractions

Convert the improper fraction $\frac{17}{10}$ to a mixed number. (Remember: an improper fraction has a numerator that is larger than the denominator.)

	Mixed Number	Working out
$\frac{17}{10}$	$1\frac{7}{10}$	$\frac{17}{10} = \frac{10}{10}$ and $\frac{7}{10}$

Convert these improper fractions to mixed numbers.

	Mixed Number	Working out
$\frac{19}{10}$	$1\frac{9}{10}$	$\frac{19}{10} = \frac{10}{10}$ and $\frac{9}{10}$
$\frac{15}{7}$	$2\frac{1}{7}$	$\frac{15}{7} = \frac{7}{7} + \frac{7}{7}$ and $\frac{1}{7}$
$\frac{10}{3}$	$3\frac{1}{3}$	$\frac{10}{3} = \frac{3}{3} + \frac{3}{3} + \frac{3}{3}$ and $\frac{1}{3}$
$\frac{23}{15}$	$1\frac{8}{15}$	$\frac{23}{15} = \frac{15}{15}$ and $\frac{8}{15}$
$\frac{49}{8}$	$6\frac{1}{8}$	$\frac{49}{8} = \frac{8}{8} + \frac{8}{8} + \frac{8}{8} + \frac{8}{8} + \frac{8}{8} + \frac{8}{8}$ and $\frac{1}{8}$
$\frac{51}{6}$	$8\frac{3}{6} = 8\frac{1}{2}$	$\frac{51}{6} = \frac{6}{6} + \frac{6}{6} + \frac{6}{6} + \frac{6}{6} + \frac{6}{6} + \frac{6}{6} + \frac{6}{6} + \frac{6}{6}$ and $\frac{3}{6}$

You may need to explain to children exactly what an improper fraction is and how it can be converted into a mixed number. The example of converting $\frac{17}{10}$ into one whole 1, made of $\frac{10}{10}$, with a remainder of $\frac{7}{10}$ should make this clear.

Number lines ☆

Write these fractions in the right places on the number line.

$\frac{3}{4}$ $\frac{7}{10}$ $\frac{4}{5}$ $\frac{11}{20}$ $\frac{17}{20}$ $\frac{1}{2}$ $\frac{1}{4}$

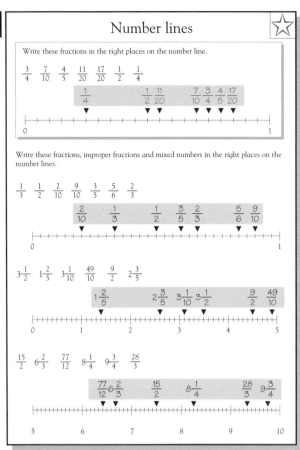

Write these fractions, improper fractions and mixed numbers in the right places on the number lines.

$\frac{1}{3}$ $\frac{1}{2}$ $\frac{2}{10}$ $\frac{9}{10}$ $\frac{3}{5}$ $\frac{5}{6}$ $\frac{2}{3}$

$3\frac{1}{2}$ $1\frac{2}{5}$ $3\frac{1}{10}$ $\frac{49}{10}$ $\frac{9}{2}$ $2\frac{3}{5}$

$\frac{15}{2}$ $6\frac{2}{3}$ $\frac{77}{12}$ $8\frac{1}{4}$ $9\frac{3}{4}$ $\frac{28}{3}$

Number lines provide a very easy way of comparing the value of different fractions and mixed numbers. Extend this exercise by creating your own number lines and groups of fractions and mixed numbers to position on them.

☆ Multiplying by units

Work out each answer.

456 × 6	823 × 8	755 × 9
2736	6584	6795

Work out each answer.

394 × 7	736 × 7	827 × 8	943 × 9
2758	5152	6616	8487

643 × 6	199 × 6	821 × 7	547 × 8
3858	1194	5747	4376

501 × 7	377 × 8	843 × 8	222 × 9
3507	3016	6744	1998

471 × 9	223 × 8	606 × 6	513 × 7
4239	1784	3636	3591

Work out each answer.

A crate holds 550 apples. How many apples will there be in 8 crates?
4400 apples

550 × 8 = 4400

A swimming pool can hold a maximum of 760 people. What is the maximum number that can visit the pool in 5 sessions?
3800 people

760 × 5 = 3800

These problems use slightly larger numbers to multiply with but the method remains the same. Make sure the child is using times tables properly or the final answer will be incorrect.

Dividing by units ☆

Work out these division sums.

$180\frac{1}{2}$ — $2\overline{)361}$ $141\frac{1}{3}$ — $3\overline{)424}$ $58\frac{3}{4}$ — $4\overline{)235}$

Work out these division sums. Part of the answer has been done for you.

$206\frac{1}{2}$ — $2\overline{)413}$ $160\frac{3}{4}$ — $4\overline{)643}$ $190\frac{2}{3}$ — $3\overline{)572}$

$204\frac{1}{4}$ — $4\overline{)817}$ $101\frac{1}{2}$ — $2\overline{)203}$ $49\frac{1}{3}$ — $3\overline{)148}$

$237\frac{3}{4}$ — $4\overline{)951}$ $182\frac{1}{2}$ — $2\overline{)365}$ $66\frac{2}{3}$ — $3\overline{)200}$

Now try these.

$164\frac{3}{4}$ — $4\overline{)659}$ $132\frac{1}{2}$ — $2\overline{)265}$ $485\frac{1}{2}$ — $2\overline{)971}$

$184\frac{1}{4}$ — $4\overline{)737}$ $283\frac{2}{3}$ — $3\overline{)851}$ $50\frac{3}{4}$ — $4\overline{)203}$

$50\frac{1}{2}$ — $2\overline{)101}$ $150\frac{4}{5}$ — $5\overline{)754}$ $126\frac{3}{5}$ — $5\overline{)633}$

Write the answer in the box.

What is 563 divided by 2? $281\frac{1}{2}$ Divide 293 by 5. $58\frac{3}{5}$

What is 374 divided by 3? $124\frac{2}{3}$ Divide 767 by 4. $191\frac{3}{4}$

Most children will be comfortable with remainders. To help them get to a fraction, explain the relationship between remainder, divider, and fractional answer. Ensure they place the answer digits above the appropriate numbers in the division box.

☆ Dividing by units

Work out these division sums.

$62\frac{6}{9} = 62\frac{2}{3}$ — $9\overline{)564}$ $66\frac{1}{7}$ — $7\overline{)463}$

Work out these division sums. Part of the answer has been done for you.

$57\frac{4}{7}$ — $7\overline{)403}$ $81\frac{7}{8}$ — $8\overline{)655}$ $22\frac{7}{9}$ — $9\overline{)205}$

$82\frac{7}{9}$ — $9\overline{)745}$ $106\frac{1}{6}$ — $6\overline{)637}$ $46\frac{1}{7}$ — $7\overline{)323}$

$63\frac{7}{9}$ — $9\overline{)574}$ $71\frac{5}{6}$ — $6\overline{)431}$ $17\frac{2}{7}$ — $7\overline{)121}$

Now try these.

$87\frac{5}{6}$ — $6\overline{)527}$ $85\frac{4}{7}$ — $7\overline{)599}$ $37\frac{1}{2}$ — $8\overline{)300}$

$24\frac{1}{9}$ — $9\overline{)217}$ $44\frac{8}{9}$ — $9\overline{)404}$ $129\frac{1}{2}$ — $6\overline{)777}$

$78\frac{3}{4}$ — $8\overline{)630}$ $70\frac{1}{2}$ — $6\overline{)423}$ $122\frac{5}{7}$ — $7\overline{)859}$

Write the answer in the box.

What is 759 divided by 7? $108\frac{3}{7}$ Divide 941 by 9. $104\frac{5}{9}$

What is 463 divided by 8? $57\frac{7}{8}$ Divide 232 by 6. $38\frac{2}{3}$

The notes from the previous page apply here, but the multiplication tables used are 6, 7, 8, and 9.

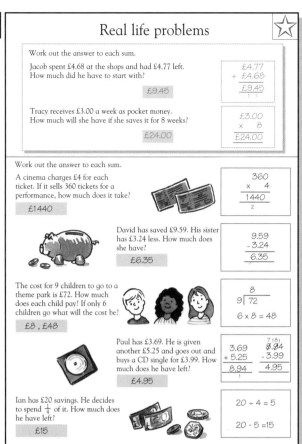

25 — Real life problems

Work out the answer to each sum.

Jacob spent £4.68 at the shops and had £4.77 left. How much did he have to start with?

£9.45

```
  £4.77
+ £4.68
  £9.45
  1 1
```

Tracy receives £3.00 a week as pocket money. How much will she have if she saves it for 8 weeks?

£24.00

```
  £3.00
×     8
  £24.00
```

Work out the answer to each sum.

A cinema charges £4 for each ticket. If it sells 360 tickets for a performance, how much does it take?

£1440

```
   360
×    4
  1440
   2
```

David has saved £9.59. His sister has £3.24 less. How much does she have?

£6.35

```
  9.59
- 3.24
  6.35
```

The cost for 9 children to go to a theme park is £72. How much does each child pay? If only 6 children go what will the cost be?

£8 , £48

```
    8
9 ) 72
6 × 8 = 48
```

Paul has £3.69. He is given another £5.25 and goes out and buys a CD single for £3.99. How much does he have left?

£4.95

```
  3.69      7 18 1
+ 5.25      8.94
  8.94    - 3.99
   1        4.95
```

Ian has £20 savings. He decides to spend ¼ of it. How much does he have left?

£15

```
20 ÷ 4 = 5
20 - 5 = 15
```

This page and page 26 provide an opportunity to apply the skills practised. Children will need to select the operation necessary. If they are unsure which operation to use, discuss whether the answer will be larger or smaller, which narrows down the options.

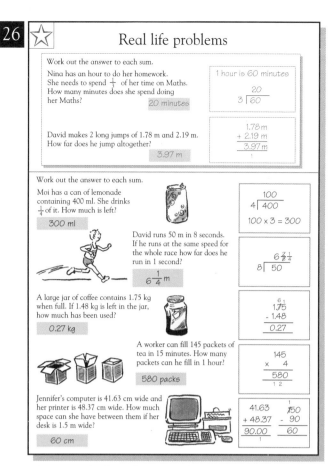

26 — Real life problems

Work out the answer to each sum.

Nina has an hour to do her homework. She needs to spend ⅓ of her time on Maths. How many minutes does she spend doing her Maths?

20 minutes

```
1 hour is 60 minutes
      20
   3 ) 60
```

David makes 2 long jumps of 1.78 m and 2.19 m. How far does he jump altogether?

3.97 m

```
  1.78 m
+ 2.19 m
  3.97 m
   1
```

Work out the answer to each sum.

Moi has a can of lemonade containing 400 ml. She drinks ¼ of it. How much is left?

300 ml

```
     100
  4 ) 400
100 × 3 = 300
```

David runs 50 m in 8 seconds. If he runs at the same speed for the whole race how far does he run in 1 second?

6 ¼ m

```
     6 2/8 1/4
  8 ) 50
```

A large jar of coffee contains 1.75 kg when full. If 1.48 kg is left in the jar, how much has been used?

0.27 kg

```
   6 1
  1.75
- 1.48
  0.27
```

A worker can fill 145 packets of tea in 15 minutes. How many packets can he fill in 1 hour?

580 packs

```
   145
×    4
   580
  1 2
```

Jennifer's computer is 41.63 cm wide and her printer is 48.37 cm wide. How much space can she have between them if her desk is 1.5 m wide?

60 cm

```
  41.63      1
+ 48.37    150
  90.00    - 90
   1         60
```

This page deals with units other than money. Note that the fifth question requires two operations to reach the answer.

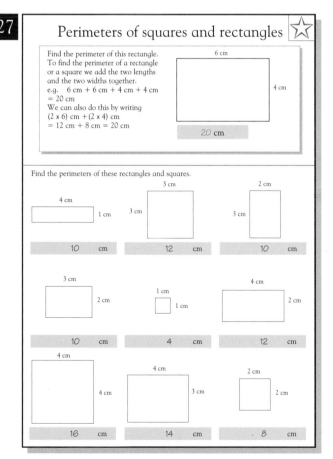

27 — Perimeters of squares and rectangles

Find the perimeter of this rectangle.
To find the perimeter of a rectangle or a square we add the two lengths and the two widths together.
e.g.   6 cm + 6 cm + 4 cm + 4 cm
= 20 cm
We can also do this by writing
(2 × 6) cm + (2 × 4) cm
= 12 cm + 8 cm = 20 cm

6 cm
4 cm

20 cm

Find the perimeters of these rectangles and squares.

4 cm, 1 cm → 10 cm
3 cm, 3 cm → 12 cm
2 cm, 3 cm → 10 cm
3 cm, 2 cm → 10 cm
1 cm, 1 cm → 4 cm
4 cm, 2 cm → 12 cm
4 cm, 4 cm → 16 cm
4 cm, 3 cm → 14 cm
2 cm, 2 cm → 8 cm

Less confident children will add the four sides. Others will multiply length and breadth by two and add them. Encourage children to see that the side of a square can be multiplied by four to reach the answer. Some may confuse perimeter and area, and multiply the sides.

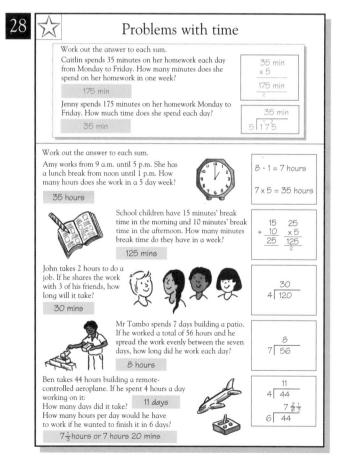

28 — Problems with time

Work out the answer to each sum.

Caitlin spends 35 minutes on her homework each day from Monday to Friday. How many minutes does she spend on her homework in one week?

175 min

```
  35 min
×      5
 175 min
   2
```

Jenny spends 175 minutes on her homework Monday to Friday. How much time does she spend each day?

35 min

```
     35 min
  5 ) 175
```

Work out the answer to each sum.

Amy works from 9 a.m. until 5 p.m. She has a lunch break from noon until 1 p.m. How many hours does she work in a 5 day week?

35 hours

```
8 - 1 = 7 hours
7 × 5 = 35 hours
```

School children have 15 minutes' break time in the morning and 10 minutes' break time in the afternoon. How many minutes break time do they have in a week?

125 mins

```
   15     25
+  10   ×  5
   25    125
          2
```

John takes 2 hours to do a job. If he shares the work with 3 of his friends, how long will it take?

30 mins

```
     30
  4 ) 120
```

Mr Tambo spends 7 days building a patio. If he worked a total of 56 hours and he spread the work evenly between the seven days, how long did he work each day?

8 hours

```
     8
  7 ) 56
```

Ben takes 44 hours building a remote-controlled aeroplane. If he spent 4 hours a day working on it:
How many days did it take?

11 days

How many hours per day would he have to work if he wanted to finish it in 6 days?

7½ hours or 7 hours 20 mins

```
      11
  4 ) 44

      7 2/3
  6 ) 44
```

For the third question check that the children divide by 4 rather than 3.

Converting units ☆

Convert 25 centimetres to milimetres.   Convert 200p to pounds.

$25 \times 10 = 250$ mm $200 \div 100 = £2$

Convert these centimetres to millimetres.

40 cm	400 mm	15 cm	150 mm	9 cm	90 mm
12 cm	120 mm	34 cm	340 mm	62 cm	620 mm
43 cm	430 mm	96 cm	960 mm	105 cm	1050 mm
92 cm	920 mm	20 cm	200 mm	426 cm	4260 mm

Convert these millimetres to centimetres.

30 mm	3 cm	100 mm	10 cm	120 mm	12 cm
60 mm	6 cm	90 mm	9 cm	200 mm	20 cm
130 mm	13 cm	10 mm	1 cm	400 mm	40 cm

Convert these pounds to pence.

£35	3500p	£600	60 000p	£15	1500p
£12	1200p	£36	3600p	£95	9500p
£72	7200p	£4	400p	£250	25 000p

Convert these pence to pounds.

450p	£4.50	900p	£9.00	6000p	£60.00
250p	£2.50	400p	£4.00	150p	£1.50
100p	£1.00	300p	£3.00	750p	£7.50

Use a ruler or money to clear out any problems with the relationship between millimetres and centimetres, and pounds and pence respectively. Watch out for answers such as £7.5. Remind that, with money, we use zero in the units column.

☆ Converting units

Convert 300 centimetres to metres.   Convert 4 kilometres to metres.

$300 \div 100 = 3$ m $4 \times 1000 = 4000$ m

Convert these centimetres to metres.

500 cm	5 m	900 cm	9 m	400 cm	4 m
8 000 cm	80 m	3 000 cm	30 m	4 000 cm	40 m
9 800 cm	98 m	8 300 cm	83 m	6 200 cm	62 m
36 800 cm	368 m	94 200 cm	942 m	73 500 cm	735 m

Convert these metres to centimetres.

47 m	4700 cm	29 m	2900 cm	84 m	8400 cm
69 m	6900 cm	24 m	2400 cm	38 m	3800 cm
146 m	14 600 cm	237 m	23 700 cm	921 m	92 100 cm

Convert these metres to kilometres.

5 000 m	5 km	6 000 m	6 km	9 000 m	9 km
15 000 m	15 km	27 000 m	27 km	71 000 m	71 km
19 000 m	19 km	86 000 m	86 km	42 000 m	42 km

Convert these kilometres to metres.

7 km	7000 m	9 km	9000 m	4 km	4000 m
23 km	23 000 m	46 km	46 000 m	87 km	87 000 m
12 km	12 000 m	96 km	96 000 m	39 km	39 000 m

Check that the child understands the relationship between centimetres and metres, and metres and kilometres. If they are secure in this understanding, this should be a straightforward page of multiplying and diving by 100 and 1 000.

Frequency table with grouped data ☆

20 children score runs in a cricket match. Here is a list of their scores: 12, 3, 3, 14, 7, 9, 19, 10, 8, 16, 8, 20, 17, 8, 7, 16, 13, 5, 12, 19. Draw the frequency table and group this data.

A class of 50 children did a science test. Here are their results: 5, 16, 6, 12, 2, 17, 19, 14, 18, 20, 18, 6, 5, 5, 4, 7, 8, 16, 9, 3, 12, 2, 14, 18, 14, 19, 4, 7, 3, 4, 20, 18, 20, 15, 20, 16, 16, 8, 15, 11, 9, 12, 16, 7, 17, 6, 9, 15, 18, 20.

Draw a frequency table to show this data.

Above is an example of how the findings could be presented. Alternatives will need to be judged carefully to decide if they are acceptable. Encourage the children to group their data and record on a tally chart. This will reduce errors in the collection of data.

☆ Rotational symmetry

What is the order of rotation of this shape?

The order of rotation is   6

This shape has an order of rotation of 6 because it can be turned onto itself 6 times.

What is the order of rotation of these shapes?

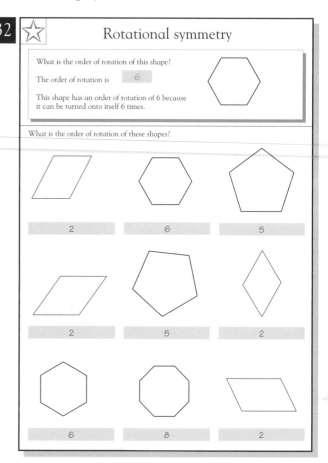

2	6	5
2	5	2
6	8	2

If the children are confused, the shapes can be traced and the tracing fitted over the original shape to show the order of rotation.